Original title:
Winter's Mirror

Copyright © 2024 Swan Charm
All rights reserved.

Author: Paula Raudsepp
ISBN HARDBACK: 978-9916-79-660-3
ISBN PAPERBACK: 978-9916-79-661-0
ISBN EBOOK: 978-9916-79-662-7

Secrets of the Snowbound Woods

In the hush of winter's breath,
Whispers curl like smoke in air.
Trees stand tall, adorned in white,
Guarding secrets, old and rare.

Footprints trace a silent path,
Through the glades of frozen breath.
Nature sleeps, a quiet heart,
Wrapped in dreams of life and death.

Frosted branches creak and sway,
Beneath the weight of crystal tears.
Every shadow seems to hold,
Stories lost across the years.

Moonlight spills on glimmering ground,
Illuminating paths untold.
Echoes dance in silver light,
While the world turns soft and cold.

In this realm where silence reigns,
Magic stirs with winter's song.
Each snowy flake, a secret kept,
In the woods where dreams belong.

Chilled Whispers Beneath the Stars

In the quiet night sky, whispers flow,
Soft secrets that only the moonlight knows.
Beneath the shivering trees, shadows play,
As stars twinkle gently, lighting the way.

Frost-kissed breezes carry tales untold,
Of dreams woven softly in silver and gold.
The air is crisp, a lullaby sweet,
Where time stands still, and echoes meet.

Glistening Shadows on Frosted Ground

Beneath a blanket of shimmering white,
Footsteps dance softly, a fleeting sight.
The world is transformed by a delicate touch,
Frosted beauty that captivates much.

Shadows stretch long, as daylight wanes,
In this frozen realm, there's peace that remains.
Every flake sparkles like dreams come alive,
In this glistening wonder, we all strive.

Icy Facade

On windows panes, the frosty art glows,
A crystalline canvas where winter flows.
Each breath is a whisper, a vaporous sigh,
Reflecting the world as the cold winds sigh.

Masks of ice cover what once shone bright,
Beneath the façade, warmth hides from the night.
Yet within the chill, embers quietly burn,
A hope for the spring, when the seasons turn.

The Stillness Between Flurries

In the heart of the storm, a moment unfolds,
Where silence envelops and magic beholds.
Snowflakes twirl gently, caught in a spin,
In the stillness of now, all chaos begins.

Time slows to a hush, each flake a soft kiss,
In this tranquil space, find a fleeting bliss.
Awaken the spirit that dances within,
In the pause of the flurry, new dreams begin.

The Quiet Spectacle

Under the moon's soft gaze,
Stars twinkle in silence,
Whispers of night unfold,
Magic in the stillness.

Trees stand as sentinels,
Draped in velvet shadows,
Time seems to pause here,
Nature's breath a secret.

The gentle breeze sighs low,
Carrying distant dreams,
Every leaf a story,
In the quiet spectacle.

Solitude in Snowfall

Soft flakes drift from above,
Blanketing the earth in white,
Silence reigns in the air,
Peace found in the cold night.

Footprints are lost to time,
A world wrapped in cotton,
Every corner whispers hope,
In solitude, forgotten.

Frosted windows glimmer bright,
Heartbeats echo within,
Wrapped in warm embrace,
The snowfall calming din.

Ethereal Hues

Sunrise spills golden light,
Painting clouds with soft blush,
Day awakens in color,
Nature's grand, gentle hush.

Mountains wear pastel crowns,
Rivers shimmer like glass,
A palette from the heavens,
In beauty's vibrant class.

Every petal a whisper,
Leaves dance in soft twilight,
Ethereal hues surround,
In day's gracefully flight.

Dance of the Flakes

Winter's breath takes the stage,
Twisting forms in the air,
Flakes pirouette and swirl,
In a frosty affair.

They gather in a flurry,
Waltzing down to the ground,
Each one a unique story,
In their soft, silent sound.

Nature's dance on display,
A show of pure delight,
Whirling, twirling in cold,
The flakes take their flight.

Frosted Reflections

In the morning light, so pale,
A world adorned with icy veil.
Shimmering paths of silvery white,
Whispers of winter, pure and bright.

Trees stand tall like frozen sentries,
Holding secrets in their entries.
Each branch a tale of seasons past,
Woven in frost, forever cast.

Footsteps crunch on glistening ground,
Echoes of silence all around.
Moments captured, a fleeting glimpse,
Nature's artistry, beauty's prints.

Time seems still, as cold winds blow,
Painting landscapes in soft glow.
Frosted breath in crisp air flies,
Nature's wonders, a soft surprise.

Evening falls, the colors fade,
Beneath the stars, a world displayed.
Reflections dance on surfaces clear,
In the stillness, magic appears.

Shattered Crystal Dreams

Fragments of light in a twilight haze,
Shimmering prisms set hearts ablaze.
Every shard tells a story lost,
Of wishes made and dreams embossed.

A rainbow caught in a fleeting glance,
Moments entwined in a tender dance.
Crystal whispers ride the gentle breeze,
Each note a promise, setting hearts at ease.

Windswept echoes of laughter ring,
In the fragments, memories cling.
Through shattered glass, a new dawn breaks,
Hope rekindles with each heart it wakes.

Patterns emerge from the chaos spun,
Bright as the rising, beckoning sun.
Every loss a chance to be free,
Shattered dreams hold possibilities.

With every step on this path unseen,
We weave together what might have been.
In the shards of crystal, life will gleam,
Reflecting beauty within each dream.

Silence in the Snow

Blankets of white cover the ground,
In the stillness, no voice found.
Each flake a whisper, soft and light,
Embracing the world in pure delight.

Moonlit nights bring a tranquil glow,
Guiding lost souls through the snow.
Footprints fade under the starry sky,
As secrets unfold where dreams lie.

Frozen streams hold their breath in time,
Nature's rhythm, a silent rhyme.
Breath suspended in the chilly air,
Moments linger, gentle and rare.

Wind carries wishes, soft and low,
In the silence, spirits flow.
Heartbeats echo in the quiet night,
Finding solace in winter's light.

Days drift softly, like snowflakes fall,
Wrapped in beauty, we feel it all.
The silence speaks, a lullaby sweet,
In the still of the snow, we find our beat.

Hushed Echoes of Ice

In the hush of dawn, ice takes flight,
Crystals shimmer in morning light.
Frozen lakes like mirrors reflect,
Nature's canvas, a pure architect.

With every step, the world aligns,
Echoes of footsteps, soft designs.
In the stillness, a story unfolds,
Of life's embrace in the winter's holds.

Branches sigh under weighty load,
As silence whispers along the road.
Silent watchers, the ancient trees,
Guard secrets held in the winter breeze.

The chill wraps around, a gentle hand,
Inviting hearts to understand.
In the quiet, the soul can soar,
Finding peace where the echoes roar.

As twilight descends, shadows play,
In the dance of night, dreams drift away.
Under the moon's soft, silver gaze,
Hushed echoes of ice weave through the maze.

The Frosted Surface of Reflection

Beneath the glassy sheen so bright,
A world of dreams takes flight.
Whispers of the past draw near,
In frozen forms, we hold what's dear.

Each ripple speaks of days gone by,
Captured moments, soft as sighs.
Reflections dance in silent grace,
The frost reveals a sacred space.

Where shadows linger, light does trace,
The beauty found in quiet place.
Emotions chill, yet warmth will rise,
A testament beneath the skies.

With every spark of crisp delight,
We gather hope in fading light.
The frozen surface, still and vast,
Becomes our canvas of the past.

A Moment Captured in Ice

In crystal frames, the seconds freeze,
A fleeting glimpse, a gentle tease.
Stillness holds each precious beat,
As time concedes to cold retreat.

Within the layers, stories lie,
Soft memories that never die.
A single breath, a world so grand,
Entrusted to the winter's hand.

Glittering shards of what once was,
Frozen laughter, fleeting cause.
Each shard reflects a life well-lived,
In silence, all that love had given.

As frostbitten boughs cradle night,
We find warm solace in the light.
A moment, steady, held on tight,
Recaptured here, a pure delight.

Frigid Tides of Memory

Waves of white crash to the shore,
Each tide brings back what came before.
In icy depths, lost tales emerge,
Frigid echoes, a timeless surge.

A chill that bites, yet stirs the soul,
Each past embrace a whispered toll.
Caught in the swell, we sail again,
Among the ghosts of where we've been.

The froth of years beneath our feet,
Unearths the moments, bittersweet.
In every crest, a flash of light,
A dance of shadows, dark and bright.

And as the tide recedes once more,
It leaves behind what we adore.
Frigid memories, deep as dreams,
Flowing through life in silent streams.

Lattice of Snowflakes

Intricate patterns, nature's art,
A dance of light, a frozen heart.
Each flake unique, a wondrous sight,
Falling softly, pure delight.

Upon the ground, they weave a tale,
In delicate threads, they subtly sail.
A tapestry of winter's song,
Where beauty thrives, no note is wrong.

The lattice formed by gentle hands,
Across the hills and quiet lands.
Each crystal twirls, a fleeting dream,
In chilly air, they softly gleam.

A symphony of white and blue,
They whisper secrets, fresh and true.
In frozen dance, they celebrate,
The art of winter, a cherished state.

Beneath the Shroud of Ice

In the embrace of winter's breath,
Silence lingers, a quiet death.
Trees stand tall, their branches bare,
Nature whispers, a chilling prayer.

Footsteps crunch on frosty ground,
Echoes lost, nowhere found.
Shadows dance in pale moonlight,
A world shrouded, hidden from sight.

Icicles hang like crystal spears,
Time suspended, frozen years.
The air is sharp, a biting chill,
Yet in this stillness, hearts can fill.

Veils of white, so soft and deep,
Secrets buried, no more to keep.
Underneath the shroud of ice,
Life awaits, a silent reprise.

Frigid Reflections

In ponds where winter winds sweep low,
Mirrors glisten, a sparkling show.
Frigid reflections in icy guise,
Whisper tales as daylight dies.

Clouded thoughts like mist arise,
Caught between the earth and skies.
Each ripple tells of dreams sought,
In the stillness, battles fought.

The sun dips low, a fading glow,
Casting shadows on the snow.
Crystals spark with a gentle prance,
Inviting all to join the dance.

Beneath the frost, life plays its tune,
Arcane notes of night and noon.
Frigid reflections, serene, sublime,
Echoing through the corridors of time.

Glimmering Traces of Solitude

A path unfolds in snowy white,
Each step marked, a fleeting sight.
Footprints linger, then they fade,
Glimmering traces, memories laid.

The world is hushed, a sacred space,
Where solitude finds its gentle grace.
Brittle branches, a fragile bow,
Holding whispers of a solemn vow.

In the stillness, silence sings,
Carrying hope on fragile wings.
Stars peek through the frozen veil,
A cosmic dance, a timeless tale.

Nature breathes in shades of white,
A canvas drawn in the quiet night.
Glimmering traces where hearts may roam,
Finding warmth in the chill of home.

Veil of the Snowy Night

The night descends, so pure, so bright,
Wrapped in the veil of snowy light.
Figures roam with ghostly grace,
Lost in dreams, a tranquil place.

Winds weave songs through distant trees,
A symphony that stirs the freeze.
Footfalls echo on frozen ground,
Whispers linger, then rebound.

Each flake dances in frosty air,
An artful waltz, beyond compare.
Silver shadows embrace the ground,
As secrets wait to be unbound.

Beneath the whisper of moonlit dreams,
Light softly falls in silver streams.
Veil of the snowy night bestows,
A hush where only silence grows.

Snowy Reveries

Whispers weave through the silent night,
Snowflakes dance in soft moonlight.
Blankets of white on slumber rest,
Nature's hush feels like a quest.

Footprints fade on the icy ground,
In this world, magic is found.
The stars twinkle in velvet skies,
Frost-kissed dreams and lullabies.

Crisp air carries a scent so pure,
In winter's arms, we feel the cure.
Timeless moments etched in glow,
Every breath, like powdered snow.

Echoes linger in the stillness there,
Memories wrapped in frosty air.
Each branch a tale of days gone by,
Snowy reveries beneath the sky.

As dawn breaks with a golden hue,
The landscape whispers soft and true.
In the heart of winter's embrace,
We find warmth in this sacred space.

Chilling Echoes

In twilight's grasp, shadows fall slow,
Frosty winds murmur secrets we know.
Beneath the stars, a chill takes flight,
Inviting whispers of the night.

Branches creak with timeless sighs,
Lost in the void, where silence lies.
Each breath clouded in the cold air,
Chilling echoes fade with despair.

Moonlight shimmers on frozen streams,
Reflections blur like fading dreams.
Paths untraveled, where memories wane,
Through the stillness, we bear the pain.

Haunted by shadows that never sleep,
Into the night, our thoughts run deep.
Each gust a shiver, a ghostly trace,
As chilling echoes reveal their grace.

The world stands still, caught in ice,
Whispers lament with each sacrifice.
In this cold, we find our way,
Guided by echoes where heartstrings sway.

Specter of Solitude

In quiet corners, shadows creep,
The specter of solitude begins to seep.
Echoes linger in empty halls,
Faint memories as silence calls.

Loneliness drapes like an old coat,
Worn threads unravel, heavy with hope.
Each sigh holds a story untold,
A heart that beats, but feels so cold.

Beneath the stars, a single light,
Flickers softly through the night.
A whispered prayer, a gentle plea,
Yearning for love to set us free.

In the stillness, we learn to cope,
Chasing shadows in search of hope.
Each heartbeat knits the fabric our own,
In the specter of solitude, we're not alone.

From within the depths, strength will rise,
With fragile wings, we touch the skies.
And in the silence, we learn to see,
The beauty of what it means to be.

Haunting Landscapes

The mist rolls in on a gray dawn,
Phantoms of dreams linger till they're gone.
Brush strokes of nature create the scene,
Haunting landscapes, where we've been.

Mountain peaks kiss the swirling clouds,
Draped in silence, they soften the louds.
Every valley holds a whispered tale,
In the stillness, we learn to prevail.

Shadows dance on the river's flow,
Reflecting lives we used to know.
Through tangled woods and fields of gold,
Haunting landscapes cradle our souls.

Crimson skies bleed into the night,
As stars awaken, shimmering bright.
Each glance back paints the past with care,
In haunting landscapes, our hearts lay bare.

Time brushes by in shades of gray,
Yet echoes of life stay bright as day.
In these vistas, we find our grace,
A haunting beauty, a sacred place.

Shiver in the Glow

Softly the twilight falls,
Amidst the chill of night.
Flickering shadows dance,
In the warmth of the light.

Whispers of winter breeze,
Kissing cheeks that are red.
Glowing fire's embrace,
A comfort for the dread.

Frosty breath drifts away,
In the laughter we share.
Hearts wrapped in cozy warmth,
Beyond the cold, a care.

Starlit skies above,
Sparkle with shining dreams.
Underneath the vastness,
Hope is more than it seems.

Together we will stand,
In this fragile delight.
Holding close what we have,
In the shiver of night.

Solstice Portraits

Winter holds her breath,
In a canvas of white.
Silent moments linger,
Captured in the light.

Dancing shadows play,
On the purest of skies.
Each breath is a story,
In winter's sweet disguise.

Colors of the dawn,
Painted with tender hues.
Time stands still between,
The old year and the new.

Eager footsteps crunch,
On the fresh fallen snow.
Whispers of the earth,
In the cold winds that blow.

Memories are woven,
In the fabric of air.
Solstice portraits tell us,
Of moments we all share.

Breath of the Cold

Glistening frost on leaves,
Whispers of morning light.
A tender chill invades,
With the dawn's early bite.

Mountains wear a blanket,
Of shimmering fine snow.
Nature breathes out slowly,
In a graceful tableau.

Footsteps crunch like glass,
In the wide-open space.
Each step a heartbeat,
In this frozen embrace.

Tempest or tranquility,
Only silence remains.
In the breath of the cold,
Life and peace intertwines.

Echoes of the wild,
In a world all our own.
We find warmth in the chill,
In the coldness overthrown.

Echoes Beneath the Ice

Beneath a fragile sheet,
Secrets lie asleep.
Echoes from the deep,
In their silence, keep.

Rippling water's song,
Dances through the freeze.
Soft murmurs of the past,
Flowing with the breeze.

Nature's hidden heart,
Beats with a gentle grace.
In the quietude,
Time finds its own pace.

Memories entangled,
In the stillness confined.
Echoes of laughter ring,
In the depths of the mind.

As seasons twist and turn,
Life returns, unfolds.
Beneath the ice, we learn,
That the warmth each heart holds.

Silent Transformation

In the quiet night, soft snow falls,
Whispers of change in silent thralls.
Nature dressed in a crystal gown,
   Hiding colors, turning brown.

Footsteps echo on paths untried,
Lost in dreams, where hopes reside.
   Gentle breath of winter's chill,
   Awakening time, a subtle thrill.

Trees stand tall, their branches bare,
More than stillness hangs in the air.
   Each flake a story from above,
   A tale of sorrow, loss, and love.

   Under moonlight's soft embrace,
   Time moves on in quiet grace.
   Silent whispers cloak the day,
   Transforming life in a new way.

Warmth encroaches, spring will call,
   Embers of life that never fall.
   Yet for now, let silence reign,
   In transformation's gentle pain.

Threads of Frost

Dewdrops cling to blades of grass,
Nature's jewels, forged to last.
Morning's breath, a chilly song,
Winter whispers, wise and strong.

Bare trees weave a tale of light,
Frosted patterns, pure and white.
Each thread glistens in the sun,
A fleeting moment, beauty spun.

Colors fade to muted hues,
Art in stillness, softest blues.
Chill invites a slower pace,
Time stands still, a warm embrace.

Icicles hang, dripped from above,
Silent sentinels, tales of love.
In every shard, reflections deep,
Secrets held, while others sleep.

As dusk falls, shadows play,
Threads of frost begin to sway.
A gentle dance, the night takes hold,
Stories whispered, waiting to unfold.

Haiku of Chill

White blankets of snow,
Quiet world, whispers unfurl,
Breath of winter's chill.

Moonlight on still ponds,
Reflections of a cold heart,
Peace in frozen dreams.

Time drips like icicles,
Moments carved in frost's embrace,
Silence speaks of hope.

Trees adorned in crystal,
Beauty wrapped in chilly air,
Nature's calm prevail.

Echoes of the night,
Softly spun in silver threads,
Winter breathes a sigh.

Winter's Elegy

In the fading light, day recedes,
Whispers of frost in empty reeds.
Nature dons a solemn shroud,
Echoes mingle, soft yet loud.

Underneath the heavy sky,
Stillness drapes where shadows lie.
Branches reach, a silent plea,
Life awaits, longing to be.

Frosty breath of dusk descends,
Time suspends as daylight ends.
Each flake a note in winter's tune,
Melodies of cold and moon.

Crackling fires draw us near,
A warmth that crowds our deepest fear.
Yet outside, the chill persists,
Fleeting moments turn to mist.

Winter's grip may feel like loss,
Yet beneath, green sprouts embossed.
In each farewell, a promise lies,
Spring will awaken, as darkness dies.

Glacial Tales

Beneath the icy peaks they lie,
Whispers of ancient winds up high.
Stories sculpted in frozen skies,
Echoes of time that never dies.

Cracks and crevices tell their part,
Drawing the curious, sparking the heart.
Each shard of ice a tale unfolds,
In the chill, a moment holds.

Blue horizons kissing the night,
Stars above shimmering bright.
Nature's canvas, vast and cold,
Every glimmer a truth retold.

Silent sentinels, proud and tall,
Guardians of the winter's thrall.
Footprints left in powdery snow,
Mark the path where wanderers go.

With every gust, the stories breathe,
In frozen realms, dreams we weave.
Glacial tales in whispers shared,
Across the ages, life declared.

The Frosted Palette

Brushstrokes of winter paint the land,
A canvas touched by nature's hand.
Silver whispers, delicate and fine,
Coating the earth in glistening line.

Shadows dance on a frosted lake,
Rippling reflections, memories wake.
The artistry born of ice and light,
Crafting beauty in the quiet night.

Pines adorned in crystal white,
Stand majestic, a breathtaking sight.
Each flake a wonder, pure and bright,
Creating a scene of pure delight.

Footsteps crunch on freshly laid ground,
Every sound a soft hallowed sound.
Nature's symphony, gentle and clear,
In frosted hues, winter draws near.

With every dawn, the palette shifts,
Colors emerge as daylight lifts.
A world reborn in sparkling lace,
The frost's embrace, a captivating grace.

Icy Embrace

Wrapped in winter's tender hold,
A whisper soft, a kiss so bold.
The world transforms in shimmering hue,
In icy embrace, all feels new.

Branches heavy with diamonds bright,
Glisten like stars in the deep of night.
Frozen rivers glide, serene,

Carrying dreams, tranquil and clean.

Gentle flurries dance in the air,
A soft touch, a lover's care.
Each flake a memory sent from above,
Carpet of white, wrapped in love.

In frozen moments, time stands still,
Hearts grow warm, a shared thrill.
As snowflakes fall, we intertwine,
In icy embrace, our spirits align.

Every breath forms a cloud of grace,
Breathless pauses, we find our place.
In this moment, together we stay,
In winter's arms, we've found our way.

Morning Crystals

Dawn emerges with blush and flair,
A tapestry woven in crisp morning air.
Each crystal glimmers in golden light,
Awakening day with a sparkling sight.

The world adorned in frost's sweet kiss,
Nature's design, a moment of bliss.
Every breath a cloud, soft and white,
Whispers of magic in the gentle light.

Breezes carry tales of the night,
Glistening branches in pure daylight.
An orchestra of silence unfolds,
Morning crystals, the stories told.

As shadows retreat, the warmth arrives,
Every heartbeat a song that thrives.
In this canvas, life starts anew,
In morning's glow, dreams come true.

Together we wander, hearts in sync,
With every step, we pause and think.
In the light, our spirits soar,
Morning crystals whisper, forevermore.

A Canvas of White

Snowflakes dance in gentle light,
Covering earth, a tranquil sight.
Whispers of winter grace the trees,
Nature's sculptor, with playful ease.

Blankets cozy, pure as lace,
Softly resting in every space.
Footprints mark a fleeting trail,
Stories told where dreams prevail.

Children laugh, with cheeks aglow,
Building castles in the snow.
Snowmen stand with hats askew,
Guardians of a world anew.

Frosted branches touch the sky,
As winter's breath begins to sigh.
In this moment, time stands still,
A canvas white, our hearts to fill.

The Breath of a Frozen Dawn

In the hush of early light,
Frosty air, a crisp delight.
Shadows stretch as sun breaks through,
Embers of warmth, a golden hue.

Birds awaken, sweet notes play,
Breaking silence of the day.
Mcrystal rivers softly gleam,
Reflecting hopes, a waking dream.

Glistening fields in silence lie,
Beneath the vast, unchanging sky.
The breath of dawn, so pure and clear,
Whispers secrets only we hear.

Footsteps crunch on frosted ground,
Echoes of nature's tranquil sound.
With open hearts, we brave the chill,
Embracing peace that lingers still.

Each moment wrapped in wonder's glow,
A frozen dawn, life's gentle flow.
In these hours, we find our grace,
Nature's beauty, our warm embrace.

Gleam of the Cold Moon

Night unfolds, a silver sheet,
Whispers soft, the stars retreat.
Moonlight bathes the world in glow,
Casting shadows, soft and slow.

The cold moon watches from above,
Shining down with tranquil love.
Silent guardians, the trees stand tall,
In this quiet, we hear their call.

Crickets sing their lullabies,
Underneath the darkened skies.
Whispers of dreams drift far and wide,
Carried gently on the tide.

In the stillness, hearts find peace,
Under the moonlight, sorrows cease.
Embracing stillness, chasing fears,
Gleaming hope through endless years.

With each glance at the night's bright face,
We find our place in time and space.
The cold moon's gleam, a guide so true,
Holding secrets old yet new.

Nature's Glassy Palette

Ponds reflect the azure skies,
Mirroring clouds as they drift by.
Nature paints with colors vast,
A vibrant blend of future and past.

Leaves shimmer in the golden rays,
While streams dance through the wooded ways.
A canvas rich with greens and gold,
Stories of the earth unfold.

Petals brush against the breeze,
In every corner, magic frees.
Dewdrops glisten on thirsty blooms,
Whispers of joy as spring resumes.

Mountains wear a cloak of white,
Beneath the sun, they gleam so bright.
Nature's palette, ever bold,
A masterpiece, priceless and gold.

In every color, every hue,
Life's rich tapestry comes to view.
Nature's glassy palette sings,
A symphony of life, it brings.

Celestial Snowfall

Soft whispers from the sky,
Falling flakes like dreams on high.
Nature drapes in white embrace,
Silent beauty, time and space.

Laughter dances in the air,
Children spin without a care.
Each flake swirls like a gentle kiss,
A fleeting moment, pure bliss.

The world transforms in quiet grace,
Winter's charm leaves no trace.
Footsteps crunch on frozen ground,
In this peace, joy is found.

Underneath the silvery glow,
Glowing soft, the moon will show.
Stars peek through the velvet night,
In the stillness, hearts feel light.

When dawn wakes and skies turn blue,
The landscape sparkles, fresh and new.
Celestial snowfall, pure delight,
A wonderland, a dream in sight.

Still Waters of Ice

Mirror-like, the lake does gleam,
Reflecting all, a tranquil dream.
Whispers of the cold winds blow,
Still waters hide what we don't know.

Edges glazed in silver sheen,
Fragile beauty, nature's scene.
A realm where time seems to freeze,
In this hush, the heart finds ease.

Frosted branches bow with grace,
Nature's calm, a soft embrace.
Beneath the ice, the world sleeps tight,
Waiting for the spark of light.

The sun dips low, a golden hue,
Painting whispers in twilight blue.
In this stillness, dreams arise,
Underneath the vast, cold skies.

Still waters speak with gentle sighs,
Songs of winter, soft replies.
In their depths, secrets unfold,
A tranquil tale, forever told.

Glacial Moments

Time stands still in icy air,
Frozen moments, debonair.
Glistening crystals, nature's art,
Each glacial touch stirs the heart.

In the quiet, shadows play,
Chasing light throughout the day.
Echoed laughter, crisp and clear,
In this stillness, joy draws near.

Mountains rise with strength and grace,
Time-lapsed beauty, a sacred space.
Intricate layers tell a tale,
Of storms that came and winds that gale.

As daylight fades, the stars ignite,
Glacial moments hold the night.
Whispers weave through the frosty chill,
In the twilight, the world stands still.

In this realm, where dreams are spun,
Every heartbeat, every run.
Glacial moments, calm and bright,
Forever etched in silver light.

The Frozen Canvas

Snowflakes swirl like soft brush strokes,
A canvas painted, nature's hopes.
Artisans of winter's breath,
Creating beauty in quiet death.

Trees adorned in crystalline gowns,
Nature's treasures, jewel crowns.
Every branch, a work of art,
Frozen whispers, stealing hearts.

Mornings break with frosty blare,
Reflecting dreams that linger there.
Amidst the stillness, a tale unfolds,
Of magic woven in chills and colds.

Sunrise paints the world anew,
A masterpiece in softest hue.
Moments captured, time does cease,
On this canvas, feeling peace.

At twilight's touch, colors blend,
The frozen canvas, time to mend.
Every layer, rich and deep,
In winter's arms, the world will sleep.

Crystalline Memories

In the heart of winter's grace,
Reflections shimmer and embrace,
Fragments of laughter, soft and bright,
Whispering tales in the quiet night.

Echoes of joy, like soft snowfall,
Twirling gently, they rise and fall,
Moments captured in ice-cold frames,
Each a treasure, none the same.

Through frosted windows, visions gleam,
Past and present intertwined, they dream,
A tapestry woven with threads of time,
Flowing softly, a timeless rhyme.

Under moonlit skies, dreams take flight,
Crystalline memories shining bright,
Held in silence, they twinkle and dance,
In the magic of winter's trance.

Through the chill, love's warmth remains,
In the heart where memory gains,
A treasure trove of frozen bliss,
Carried in every icy kiss.

Frost-laden Frontiers

Where the world turns white under the sky,
Frosted whispers wander by,
Hidden pathways invite the bold,
To explore stories yet untold.

Crystals crunch beneath each step,
Nature's blanket, a dream adept,
Breath visible in the cold air,
Moments carved with utmost care.

Trees like statues, dressed in white,
Guarding secrets of the night,
Branches reach for the distant flames,
Echoes of warmth call their names.

Snowflakes dance on the chilly breeze,
Gentle murmurs through the trees,
Frost-laden frontiers, vast and wide,
Where dreams and nature coincide.

In this realm of silence profound,
Every heartbeat is a sound,
The beauty of a winter's glow,
Eternal paths where spirit flows.

Echoes Under a Layer of Snow

Buried deep where silence sleeps,
Echoes linger, secrets keep,
Covered whispers, soft and low,
Rest beneath a layer of snow.

Frozen laughter, shadows play,
Tales of joy in winter's sway,
Glistening dreams in nature's hold,
Messages of warmth retold.

Each flake falls, a story spun,
Tracing paths till day is done,
Fleeting moments, pure and bright,
Memories wrapped in the night.

Veils of white blanket the ground,
Where hidden echoes can be found,
A serenade of stillness reigns,
Muffled whispers, joy remains.

Beneath the hush, a heartbeat swells,
Time dances, and magic dwells,
Echoes waiting to be freed,
Under the snow, dreams proceed.

A Symphony of Stillness

In the hush of winter's breath,
Silence sings a song of depth,
A symphony of soft repose,
Where the heart's quietude grows.

Snowflakes fall like gentle notes,
Composing tunes that nature wrote,
Each delicate flake a sound,
In harmony, the world unwound.

The world in white, a tranquil scene,
Where hope and peace can intervene,
Frozen moments, beauty stilled,
In this silence, hearts are filled.

Frost-kissed air, a lullaby,
Underneath the vast, dark sky,
A dance of stillness, a spellbound trance,
In winter's song, dreams take their chance.

A call to pause, reflect, and feel,
In the stillness, truths reveal,
A symphony that softly plays,
In winter's embrace, love stays.

Crystal Dreams

In moonlit whispers, crystals gleam,
They dance like shadows in a dream.
With every glint, a story told,
Of fleeting hopes and dreams of gold.

Through sparkling skies, our wishes soar,
Adrift on winds, forevermore.
Each star above, a guiding light,
Illuminating the depths of night.

A gentle breeze, a soft embrace,
In crystal dreams, we find our place.
On silver shores of endless trusts,
We walk together, two soul's gusts.

With every sigh, the echoes ring,
In crystal dreams, we're birds in spring.
Through starlit paths, our hearts align,
In whispered wishes, love will shine.

Awake we rise to greet the dawn,
With crystal dreams, we carry on.
As day unfolds, our spirits roam,
In endless skies, we find our home.

Frigid Lullabies

In winter's grasp, the world turns still,
The night is filled with soft goodwill.
A lullaby of frost and snow,
Whispers gently, ebb and flow.

Underneath the silver glow,
Chill winds carry tales of woe.
Yet in the silence, some find peace,
In frigid songs, their worries cease.

With each note, a spirit flies,
In dreams that weave through frigid skies.
Bare branches sway, their shadows blend,
In melodies, hearts mend and bend.

The warmth of hearts, a fire's flame,
Against the cold, it calls our name.
In every breath, a silent prayer,
Frigid lullabies fill the air.

As twilight fades and stars ignite,
We find our solace in the night.
With every hush, a soft goodbye,
In frigid lullabies, we lie.

A Silence Wrapped in Ice

Cold winds whisper through the trees,
Where nature holds its breath with ease.
A silence wrapped in shrouded white,
Cloaked in shadows, lost to light.

Each flake that falls, a whispered thought,
In icy realms, our dreams are caught.
We wander through this frozen haze,
In quiet paths, our spirits blaze.

With every step upon the frost,
We find the warmth in what we've lost.
A gentle hush, the world sleeps still,
In icy realms, there's time to heal.

Beneath the cloak of winter's chill,
The heart beats on, a steady thrill.
In moments wrapped, where echoes sigh,
A silence wrapped in ice draws nigh.

As dawn approaches, hues will gleam,
This silence deep, a lucid dream.
In cold embrace, we find our way,
A world reborn with each new day.

Frost-kissed Daydreams

In morning light, both crisp and bright,
Frost-kissed petals dance in flight.
With every glow, a story sings,
Of fleeting joy and boundless springs.

Through fragrant fields where whispers sigh,
Our daydreams soar, forever high.
Each frosty breath, a wish set free,
In cerulean skies, our spirits flee.

As sunlight warms the icy dew,
We chase the dreams that feel so true.
With every step on shimmering ground,
Frost-kissed laughter can be found.

In twilight's embrace, as stars align,
We weave our tales, hearts intertwine.
With every glance, horizons gleam,
In frost-kissed daydreams, we redeem.

So let us roam, let spirits play,
In daydreams bright, where hope holds sway.
With every smile, let love ignite,
In frosted whispers, pure delight.

The Frosted Silence

Whispers dance upon the air,
A stillness clad in frosty wear.
The world sleeps beneath a quilt,
In purest white, no warmth to tilt.

Trees stand tall, their limbs adorned,
With crystals crafted, winter's crown.
Each breath escapes like fragile snow,
A hush that comforts, soft and low.

Footsteps muffled, shadows roam,
In this cold, a silent home.
Frozen echoes gently sway,
Holding secrets of the day.

As night descends, stars gleam bright,
On the frost that shimmers white.
Nature's magic, crisp and clear,
In this silence, peace draws near.

The frost collects on every pine,
A tranquil beauty so divine.
In stillness, hearts can softly learn,
In winter's grip, the world can turn.

Mirage of Ice

In a crystal land, where dreams collide,
Mirages dance, no place to hide.
Colors twirl in a fleeting trance,
An icy realm, where spirits prance.

Reflections shimmer on a glassy lake,
Each movement whispers, each shimmer wakes.
A phantom world of blue and white,
In the golden rays, it feels just right.

Glistening paths of frost don the ground,
Every step a silent sound.
A harmony of cold and light,
In this enchanted, frozen sight.

With every breath, the air is sweet,
A winter melody, soft and neat.
Morning breaks with the sun's warm kiss,
In this mirage, we find our bliss.

Days unfold in a frosted dream,
Life dances lightly, like a beam.
In this magical, snowy embrace,
We find the spirit of winter's grace.

Glinting Dawn

A new day breaks, the sky alight,
With hues of orange, pink, and white.
Glints and glimmers in the dew,
Awake the world, fresh and new.

Mountains glow in morning's arms,
Wrapped in warmth, nature charms.
Birds take flight, their songs arise,
In harmony with morning skies.

Golden rays kiss every leaf,
Bringing promise, chasing grief.
Shadows vanish, light takes hold,
In this dawn, our dreams unfold.

The air is crisp, a gentle breeze,
Whispers through the swaying trees.
Hope is stirred, as day's begun,
Glimmers dancing, life's sweet run.

With every heartbeat, life renews,
As nature plays its vibrant hues.
Glinting dawn, a painted view,
A canvas born of bright and true.

Shadows on the Snow

Footsteps trace a tale untold,
In a world of blue and gold.
Shadows stretch beneath the trees,
In winter's grasp, a gentle freeze.

Every flake a story bears,
Echoes linger, caught in snares.
The silence calls with every sway,
As shadows dance and driftaway.

The fading light, it quiets down,
Covering the earth like a gown.
Darkness wraps the day in grace,
While moonlight takes its silver place.

Stars emerge, a twinkling show,
In the depths of midnight's glow.
Whispers weave through winter's chill,
In shadows deep, the heart is still.

Tomorrow's dawn will break anew,
Fresh footprints on the morning dew.
But for now, we hold the night,
In shadows soft, a sweet delight.

Icebound Serenity

In the hush of frozen night,
Stars twinkle, shining bright.
Whispers weave through icicle trees,
A gentle sigh in the winter breeze.

Moonlight casts a silver thread,
On a blanket where dreams are spread.
Silence lingers, deep and clear,
Filling each heart with winter's cheer.

Footprints crunch on glistening ground,
In this stillness, peace is found.
Nature's grasp holds tight and strong,
In its embrace, we all belong.

Frosty breath in the air we share,
Moments of beauty, rare and fair.
Here we stand, wrapped in the glow,
Of a winter's night, soft and slow.

With every star, our hopes are drawn,
In this icebound serenity, we are reborn.

Luminescent Drift

Beneath the waves, so dark and deep,
The secrets of the ocean keep.
Bioluminescent creatures gleam,
In a mystical, watery dream.

Gentle currents swirl and play,
Guided by the moonlight's ray.
Murmmurs of the tide's sweet song,
In the depths where we belong.

Waves of light dance in embrace,
Painting shadows on the space.
A symphony beneath the sea,
In every ripple, wild and free.

Echoes of the softest sound,
Where hidden wonders float around.
A luminescent world unfolds,
Tales of beauty still untold.

Drifting through this glowing night,
We find our way, pure delight.

Soft Crystals

On the window, frost does bloom,
Patterns lace the quiet room.
Soft crystals glimmer, pure and white,
Capturing the magic of the night.

Each flake a work of art divine,
In nature's hand, a perfect line.
Delicate, they shimmer, reflect,
A moment caught; we stand in respect.

In the dawn, they slowly melt,
Dreams of winter gently dealt.
Morning light with warmth brings grace,
As the crystals lose their place.

Yet in our hearts, they will remain,
The beauty of that frosty reign.
Memories of winter's kiss,
In every flake, a fleeting bliss.

So let us cherish this design,
Those soft crystals, ever divine.

The Dance of Solitude

In the quiet, shadows play,
Echoes of the day drift away.
Solitude wraps its gentle arms,
An invitation to its charms.

Steps are whispered, soft and light,
Laughter lingers in the night.
Alone yet never truly so,
In this dance, we learn to grow.

With every spin, we find our space,
In the stillness, a warm embrace.
Moments stretch in cosmic flow,
Through solitude, our spirits glow.

As stars flicker, dreams ignite,
In the shadows, we find our light.
With every turn, we weave the thread,
Of a tapestry where hearts are led.

So let us dance beneath the moon,
In solitude, we find our tune.

The Breath of an Icy Gale

Whispers through the willow trees,
A chill that stings and bites,
Nature's breath, a frosty tease,
Wrapped in shimmering lights.

Clouds drift low, a heavy gray,
Veils of mist and frost adorn,
The world asleep, in hues of clay,
In this silence, we are sworn.

Wind that howls, a haunting sound,
Each flake falls with gentle grace,
Land and sky, they intertwine,
In this frozen, timeless space.

Branches bow with jeweled weight,
A glisten hidden, pure and bright,
As shadows dance, it's never late,
To marvel at the spellbound night.

Echoes linger in the air,
A moment caught in crystal gleam,
The icy breath, a fleeting prayer,
Nature's heart, a frozen dream.

Slumbering Woods in White

Blanketed in winter's hush,
Silent woods draped in snow,
Trees stand still, their limbs a brush,
Painting scenes of light's soft glow.

Footprints lost where paths once roamed,
Nature's cradle, soft and deep,
In this realm where dreams have homed,
The secrets of the stillness seep.

Frosted pines, in whispered breeze,
Glimmering stars weave through the night,
Every sound, a soft reprise,
Waking slumbering dreams in flight.

Moonlight dances on the ground,
Casting shadows, pure and bright,
In the silence, peace is found,
Wrapped within the arms of night.

A blanket soft, the world reclaims,
In white, the earth, a quiet sigh,
With every breath, the silence flames,
In slumber, time seems to fly.

Frozen Echoes of Time

In the stillness, echoes freeze,
Moments caught like breath in air,
Ghosts of laughter in the breeze,
Whispers linger, ever rare.

Icicles hang like memories,
Sharp and clear, yet fragile too,
Time suspended, stories tease,
In crystal shapes, a world anew.

Fields adorned in snowy shrouds,
Frosty blankets, pure and wide,
Nature's canvas, soft and proud,
Holding secrets time can't hide.

Tales of ages etched in ice,
Footprints of those that came before,
Each sharp breath, a bold device,
To capture moments to explore.

Silent call of winter's breath,
Through the woods, the echoes wind,
In the space between life and death,
Frozen echoes, sweetly kind.

Crystals in the Stillness

Glistening gems in fading light,
Each droplet hangs, a world contained,
Reflections dance, a pure delight,
In stillness, beauty unchained.

Crisp air filled with winter's song,
As silence wraps the earth's embrace,
Moments here, where time feels long,
Awakening a timeless space.

Frosted leaves like fragile lace,
Delicate in their quiet grace,
Whispers lost in nature's face,
Each crystal tells a story's trace.

Beneath the sky of twilight's blend,
Stars appear, a twinkling seam,
In every crystal, joys extend,
Reflecting hopes, a winter dream.

Softly falling, there they lay,
In silent beauty, pure and bright,
Crystals gathered, winter's play,
In stillness, hearts take flight.

Chilling Reverie

Whispers float on winter's breath,
Dreams are frozen, time is still.
Night unfolds a silver sheath,
Moonlight dances on the hill.

Fields adorned in icy lace,
Branches glisten, soft and bright.
In this calm, we find our place,
Wrapped in warmth, embraced by night.

A gentle hush, the world at rest,
Solitude's sweet, tender song.
In the frosty air, we're blessed,
Hearts aligned, where we belong.

Stars above like diamonds gleam,
Nature's canvas, pure and wide.
In this moment, we can dream,
Side by side, we'll bide our time.

With every breath, we share a wish,
For the thaw that breaks this chill.
But in this peace, there's much to relish,
In frost's embrace, our souls are still.

Frosted Landscapes

Crystals spark on fields of white,
A blanket soft, a whispered sigh.
Footprints mark the morning light,
Nature's wonder, I walk by.

Trees adorned in shimmering frost,
Each branch clothed in icy hue.
In this beauty, we know no loss,
Every moment feels so new.

Rivers slow, a mirror clear,
Reflecting all the world's delight.
In this scene, we hold what's dear,
Just me and you, the stars ignite.

Winds will sing a winter's tune,
As we wander hand in hand.
Beneath the watchful, glowing moon,
In frosted landscapes, we will stand.

Each breath we take, a cloud of white,
In this magic, hearts entwine.
The world feels vast, serene, and bright,
In winter's arms, we softly shine.

A Quiet Reflection

In stillness, echoes softly play,
Silent thoughts drift through the air.
The night adorns a velvet gray,
As stars awaken, unaware.

Reflections dance upon the lake,
Mirroring the moon's embrace.
In tranquil depths, we find we wake,
And lose ourselves in time and space.

A canopy of shimmering light,
Wraps the world in a gentle fold.
Each moment holds a heart so bright,
As secrets whisper, untold.

With every breath, the quiet sings,
A lullaby of nature's grace.
In solitude, the spirit clings,
To brighter dreams we now can chase.

So let us linger in this peace,
Where worries fade, and joys arise.
In quiet reflection, hearts find ease,
Underneath the starlit skies.

Melodies of the Frost

Notes of winter fill the air,
A symphony of dreams untold.
Softly, gently, without a care,
The chill wraps us in its hold.

Harmonies of whispers near,
Frosted branches sway to the song.
In every flake, a world appears,
Delicate, yet bold and strong.

Underneath the moonlit glow,
The earth begins to hum along.
In frosty breaths, our laughter flows,
Creating tunes where we belong.

So dance with me in winter's grace,
As melodies entwine and spin.
In every step, our hearts embrace,
The music of the frost within.

With every note, let worries flee,
In this moment, time stands still.
A cherished song, just you and me,
In winter's arms, love's perfect thrill.

Enchanted by the Glaze

A shimmer drapes the evening light,
In whispers soft, the world takes flight.
Each crystal flake a dream unfurls,
In nature's dance, a swirl of pearls.

The branches wear their icy crown,
As twilight settles softly down.
Each breeze a song, a gentle sigh,
In shadows deep where fairies lie.

Footprints trace a path anew,
Underneath the skies so blue.
A magic thread weaves through the air,
An enchanted spell beyond compare.

With every breath, the moment glows,
While time around us gently slows.
In frosty breath, we find our grace,
In every smile, in every place.

Let laughter ring and warmth ignite,
As stars awaken in the night.
In shimmering lights, our spirits rise,
Enchanted by the glaze of skies.

Beneath the White Veil

A quiet hush envelops all,
As snowflakes dance and softly fall.
Beneath this veil of purest white,
The world is wrapped in soft delight.

Amidst the trees, the silence reigns,
As winter whispers in gentle chains.
Each branch a poem, silently penned,
In nature's book, on it depend.

The hearths are warm, the laughter flows,
In cozy corners, love brightly glows.
Beneath the white, the heart finds peace,
In moments sweet that never cease.

Time gently drifts like the falling snow,
With every flake, our worries go.
A tapestry woven, soft and deep,
Beneath the veil, our secrets keep.

As morning breaks, the world is bright,
A masterpiece in purest light.
We gather close, our spirits swell,
In beauty found beneath the spell.

Twilight in the Frost

The sun dips low, the shadows grow,
In frosted fields where whispers flow.
Twilight drapes its velvet cloak,
In silence deep, the dreams awoke.

The moon ascends with silver beams,
Illuminating fragile dreams.
Each crystal twinkle, bright and clear,
Embracing all that's held so dear.

A frostbitten breath, the air so crisp,
As twilight sways in nature's lisp.
With every step, the world shines bright,
A dance of stars in velvet night.

Nestled close, the hearts entwine,
In this embrace, the world feels fine.
The twilight hums a soothing tune,
A serenade beneath the moon.

With every heartbeat, we are bound,
In this magic, life is found.
Twilight in the frost, we find,
The warmth of love, forever kind.

Ethereal Hues of Hibernation

In slumber deep, the earth lies still,
Wrapped in whispers of winter's chill.
Ethereal hues paint the land,
As dreams of spring go hand in hand.

A canvas wide, in blues and greys,
Where sunlight dims, the heart obeys.
In quiet corners, shadows play,
In hibernation's soft ballet.

Life beneath the surface stirs,
Preparing for the song of birds.
With every pulse, a promise grows,
In time, the vibrant life bestows.

The world at peace in stillness finds,
A gentleness that soothes our minds.
In these hues, our spirits blend,
As we await the warmth to trend.

So let the season's song unfold,
In hues of blue and stories told.
For in this rest, the seeds will sow,
Ethereal dreams that soon will glow.

Echoes of the Solstice

The sun dips low in golden haze,
As shadows stretch on twilight's face.
Whispers of warmth in fading light,
Embrace the edge of winter's night.

Nature breathes in calm repose,
Time stands still as twilight grows.
A dance of light and darkness blends,
In this moment, silence tends.

Stars awaken, twinkling bright,
Casting dreams on the cloak of night.
Echoes of joy, a soft refrain,
Resounding through the crisp terrain.

The world slows down, the heart knows peace,
In solstice' grip, all worries cease.
With each heartbeat, nature's song,
Reminds us where we all belong.

As seasons shift, let spirits rise,
In echoes found beneath the skies.
Together, united we find our way,
Within the warmth of a faded day.

Beneath the Frost

A blanket white on slumbering ground,
Silent whispers weave all around.
Beneath the frost, the earth holds tight,
Dreaming of blooms in spring's delight.

Branches bare, adorned with ice,
Nature's jewels, a glistening slice.
Each breath a cloud in the chilling air,
Echoing softly, a prayer laid bare.

Crystals dance in the morning sun,
A fleeting moment, a day begun.
Each step a crunch on the powdery bed,
As life beneath stirs, softly fed.

In frozen stillness, secrets reside,
Life waits patiently, deep inside.
For soon the thaw, the warmth will gleam,
Awakening all from winter's dream.

Beneath the frost, hope softly glows,
A promise woven in nature's prose.
Through icy veils, life's hand will trace,
The beauty wrapped in winter's grace.

Tranquil Whispers

In quiet woods where shadows play,
Tranquil whispers gently sway.
Leaves converse in muted tones,
Secrets shared among the stones.

A brook babbles, a serenade,
Through the glen where dreams cascade.
Amidst the pines, a soft embrace,
Awakens peace in nature's face.

Sunbeams filter through the trees,
Kissing petals, dancing leaves.
The world slows in this sacred space,
Time stands still, a warm embrace.

Gentle breezes breathe and sigh,
Like old friends who linger nigh.
In every rustle, a story unfolds,
Of days gone by and wisdom shared.

Here, in stillness, hearts align,
Finding solace, pure and divine.
Tranquil whispers, soft and light,
Guide our souls through day and night.

Ethereal Reflection

In still waters, the stars descend,
Mirroring dreams where ripples blend.
Ethereal whispers float like mist,
A dance of light that can't be missed.

Moonlit shadows sway and glide,
Embracing secrets the night can't hide.
Reflections shimmer in silent pools,
Telling tales of forgotten jewels.

As breezes tease the surface calm,
Nature's breath, a soothing balm.
In twilight's cradle, the heart expands,
Gathering hope in silken hands.

Stars twinkle down, a guiding grace,
Leading souls to a sacred place.
Ethereal dreams in quiet flight,
Cradle us in the arms of night.

With every glimpse, the world transforms,
In the embrace of gentle storms.
An echo of love carved in reflection,
Awakens the heart's deep connection.

Frostbitten Dreams

In the quiet night, stars gleam bright,
Dreams wrapped in frost, a chilling flight,
Whispers of winter, gentle and soft,
Carried on breezes, aloft and lost.

Fields of snow where shadows lay,
Frozen hopes in a deep array,
Each breath a whisper, crisp and clear,
Frostbitten dreams, held dear and near.

The moonlight dances on icy streams,
Reflecting the light of our hidden dreams,
Nature's canvas, a shimmering sight,
Painted in hues of silver and white.

Time stands still in this serene chill,
Each moment captured, a memory still,
With every heartbeat, the frost draws near,
Frostbitten dreams that we hold dear.

Awake or asleep, the visions roam,
In a frosty world, we call our home,
Embraced by winter, so soft and deep,
Frostbitten dreams, in silence we keep.

Silent Serenade

In the hush of night, a song so sweet,
Nature sings softly, a gentle greet,
The moon overhead, casting a glow,
Whispers of wind, like secrets flow.

Branches sway lightly in winter's tune,
Under the watch of a silver moon,
Snowflakes dancing, a twinkling waltz,
Silent serenade, a heart's pulse halts.

Footprints in white, a path untold,
Leading to stories of warmth and cold,
Echoes of laughter in frosty air,
Moments remembered, a breath to share.

Stars blink above in the midnight sky,
Listening close to the world's soft sigh,
Each note a promise, a fleeting sigh,
Silent serenade, where dreams comply.

A lullaby sung by the winter's breath,
Filling the silence, defying death,
With every note, our hearts unfold,
Silent serenade, a beauty bold.

Frosty Glimpses

Through frosted glass, the world anew,
Sparkles of ice, a mystic view,
Glimpses of life wrapped in winter's veil,
Nature's artwork tells a silent tale.

Sunlight breaks through, a warming kiss,
Illuminating moments we cannot miss,
Each flake a story, a dance divine,
In frosty glimpses, our hearts entwine.

Time drips slowly, a melting sigh,
Echoes of laughter as days pass by,
In a crystal frame, we pause to see,
Frosty glimpses of you and me.

The seasons whisper, a breath of change,
Shapes of the past, so sweet and strange,
In frozen frames, the memories glisten,
Frosty glimpses, in silence they listen.

Together we stand, while time takes flight,
Bound by the magic of wintry light,
With every glance, our spirits roam,
Frosty glimpses, a winter's home.

Shattered Glass of Ice

Beneath the surface, the silence waits,
Shattered glass of ice, nature's fates,
Every crack tells a story half-spun,
Reflections of light as the day is done.

Footsteps echo on the frozen ground,
In the stillness, whispers can be found,
Life's hidden secrets in delicate lines,
Shattered glass of ice, where time aligns.

The beauty and fragility intertwined,
A dance of shadows that fate designed,
With each sharp edge, a moment to hold,
Shattered glass of ice, stories unfold.

Breath of winter, a shiver runs deep,
Nature's embrace, a promise to keep,
In the fractured light, we find our way,
Shattered glass of ice on this winter's day.

Together we venture, through cold and grace,
Finding our footing in this frozen place,
With every heartbeat, we remain bold,
Shattered glass of ice, our stories told.

Glacial Whispers

In the hush of winter's breath,
Shadows dance on icy floors.
Gentle echoes, silent depths,
Nature's secrets, softly roars.

Moonlight cradles frozen streams,
Twinkling stars in velvet skies.
Whispers weave through frosty dreams,
A chill that never truly lies.

Snowflakes kiss the barren ground,
Delicate as whispered hymns.
Each a tale that's tightly bound,
Lost in night, as daylight dims.

Frigid winds play haunting tunes,
Awakening the silent trees.
Beneath their weight, the world communes,
With stories carried on the breeze.

Time stands still in icy grace,
An artful pause, the world at rest.
In glacial whispers, find your place,
Nature's canvas, cold and blessed.

A Tapestry of Snow

A blanket soft, purest white,
Covers ground with gentle care.
Each flake, a spark of light,
Dances softly through the air.

Flurries swirl in graceful arcs,
Embroidered dreams by winter's hand.
Silent songs in starlit parks,
A wondrous quilt across the land.

Branches draped in frosty lace,
Glisten under moonlit beams.
Nature weaves a perfect space,
Where every glance ignites our dreams.

Trails of footprints, stories told,
Mark the journey through the night.
In the quiet, brave and bold,
Adventures await in the light.

A tapestry of moments spun,
In the chill of winter's breath.
Each soft snowfall, a new begun,
A fleeting masterpiece of death.

Lace of the Night

Silver threads in dark embrace,
Weave the fabric of the night.
Stars like jewels, a stellar lace,
Glimmer gently, pure delight.

Underneath this cosmic dome,
Shadows stretch, begin to play.
Whispers lure the heart back home,
In the stillness, dreams sway.

Moonbeams fall like softest dew,
Kissing life with tender care.
In the night, the world feels new,
A tranquil space, beyond compare.

Glistening paths in twilight's glow,
Invite the wanderers to roam.
With each breath, the secrets flow,
In the silence, find your home.

Nature dances, sweet and free,
In the lace of velvet night.
Wrapped in joy, let your soul be,
Awash in peace, and pure delight.

Indelible Frost

Crystals form in morning's light,
Painting windows with their art.
Each design, a fleeting sight,
Etched in time, they touch the heart.

Breath of winter, cool and bold,
Wraps the world in icy breath.
Stories whispered, tales unfold,
Underneath the touch of death.

Frosty patterns weave and twine,
On the glass, they softly play.
In their beauty, secrets shine,
Marking moments, gone away.

Glimmers of a season's span,
Indelible but brief and frail.
Nature's hand, a silent plan,
Capturing the heart's own trail.

As the sun begins to rise,
Warming all that cold had claimed.
Memories in frost remain,
Etched in time, forever named.

Veil of Ice

A whispering breeze flows so cold,
It wraps the earth in a shroud of gold.
Beneath the stars, the world will freeze,
In silence deep, it finds its peace.

Glinting, shimmering, a crystal sight,
The moon above bathes all in light.
Frozen branches arch and bow,
Time stands still, here and now.

A blanket plush, a frosty sheet,
Where nature rests, so soft, so sweet.
Each breath a cloud, a fleeting ghost,
In this frozen land, we linger most.

Footsteps whisper through the night,
Echoing softly, a quiet flight.
The veil of ice begins to glow,
In the heart of winter's show.

Yet under this beauty, so serene,
Lies a depth of the unseen.
Cold can bite, and hearts can freeze,
But still, we find our moments tease.

A Frigid Dance

Snowflakes twirl with grace and flair,
A ballet spun in crisp, cold air.
Nature sways to the winter tune,
Under the watchful eye of the moon.

Branches bow in a rhythmic sway,
Embracing the frost, come what may.
The world adorned in a sparkling coat,
As time drifts on, like a ghostly boat.

Footsteps crunch on the frosted ground,
A symphony of silence surrounds.
In every flake, a story told,
Of winter's warmth and the chill of cold.

The icy waltz of whispers near,
Each moment shared, a memory dear.
Captured still in winter's trance,
We lose ourselves in this frigid dance.

As dawn approaches, colors blend,
The end of night, an icy friend.
Yet still, we cherish the night's embrace,
For in its arms, we find our place.

Glistening Solitude

In the stillness of a winter's night,
Frosted dreams take quiet flight.
A world so vast, encased in glass,
Reflections of moments that slowly pass.

The stars above twinkle and gleam,
Like distant ships in an icy dream.
Alone we stand, yet never apart,
In nature's clutch, we find a heart.

Glistening solitude, pure and bright,
Whispers of magic dance in the light.
Each flake that falls is a soft embrace,
In the quiet hour, we find our place.

Shadows stretch beneath the trees,
Caressed by sighs of the gentle breeze.
Each breath a mist in the frosty air,
In this glistening world, we cease to care.

As dawn begins to break the spell,
We hold the night and bid farewell.
Yet in our hearts, the quiet stays,
In glistening solitude, love always plays.

Spectral Chill

A spectral chill fills the night,
Shadows dance in fleeting light.
The air is thick with whispers low,
As winter's breath begins to flow.

The world in frost, a silent scream,
Wrapped in the folds of a waking dream.
Ghostly figures, pale and bright,
Float through the remnants of fading light.

Each rustling leaf, a tale untold,
Echoes of season, both new and old.
In frosted air, we hear the call,
As spectral chill blankets all.

The moon hangs high, a watchful eye,
On moments of sorrow, moments of sigh.
Through shadows, we wander, lost and found,
In a spectral chill, life spins around.

Yet warmth resides in every heart,
Binding us close, though we're apart.
In the still of night, we draw together,
In spectral chill, we find forever.

Whispered in the Snow

Softly falls the snow, so light,
A blanket of whispers, pure and bright.
Each flake a secret, softly told,
In the hush of night, a story unfolds.

Footsteps fade on the frozen ground,
In stillness, only silence is found.
The trees stand tall, dressed in white,
Guardians of dreams in the pale moonlight.

Breezes carry the tales of the frost,
Every moment cherished, never lost.
A world transformed, serene and slow,
Magic lingering in the falling snow.

Children's laughter breaks the calm,
Building snowmen, holding warmth like a balm.
In the quiet, joy does bloom,
As nature dances in the icy room.

Whispers swirl in the chilly air,
Promises kept with tender care.
In the cradle of winter, dreams are sown,
In every flake, a love is grown.

Glistening Shadows

Evening falls, and shadows creep,
Glistening secrets, in silence they keep.
Moonlight dances on the cold ground,
A symphony of lights, without a sound.

Branches stretch, reaching for the night,
Each one a silhouette, bold and bright.
As stars emerge from the earthly shroud,
Whispers of wonder swirl all around.

Frosty breath hangs in the air,
With every moment, magic to share.
The world transforms beneath the glow,
In glistening shadows, dreams gently flow.

Footsteps echo on this frozen stage,
Wonders written page by page.
In the quiet, hearts intertwine,
In this symphony, your soul meets mine.

The night unfolds with a silver thread,
Woven stories of all that's said.
In shadows, we find our light's embrace,
Glistening softly, time slows its pace.

A World in White

A world in white, so pristine and fair,
Cloaked in silence, floating through air.
Every branch seems to hold its breath,
As beauty glimmers, defying death.

The sun peeks out, a timid gaze,
Warming the ground with gentle rays.
Nature awakens in a hushed delight,
Transforming the land with colors so bright.

Complaints of winter now fade away,
In the dance of snowflakes, hearts start to sway.
Children play, snowballs in flight,
Creating memories in the soft twilight.

Time seems to pause in this frozen dream,
Lost in laughter, we float downstream.
In a world where magic takes its stand,
We find our solace, hand in hand.

Graceful whispers in the winter's breath,
Reminding us all of life's quiet depth.
A world in white, where love can spark,
In the echoes of joy, we find our mark.

Stillness of the Season

Stillness reigns in the twilight hour,
Each flake of snow, a delicate flower.
Nature's palette, painted with care,
In the quiet moments, we find our share.

Branches bow beneath the weight,
Of winter's touch, of love and fate.
Round every corner, the whispers weave,
In the still of the night, we dare to believe.

Candles flicker in windows aglow,
Inviting warmth as the cold winds blow.
In the hearts of many, a fire ignites,
A haven of hope in the frosty nights.

Time stands still in this tranquil space,
Unraveling worries, a gentle embrace.
As stars unveil their distant dance,
We breathe in the stillness, lost in a trance.

The season of magic, a soft lullaby,
Underneath the vast and starry sky.
In the stillness, we find life's grace,
In the heart of winter, a warm embrace.

Enchanted Silence

In the woods where shadows play,
Soft whispers dance among the trees.
Moonlight weaves a silver sway,
Nature's heart begins to tease.

A gentle breeze begins to hum,
Secrets held in every sigh.
Crickets sing, the night is numb,
Stars awaken in the sky.

Beneath the boughs, dreams softly weave,
Time stands still, a sacred vow.
In this hush, we dare believe,
Magic breathes with every prow.

Amidst the dark, a lantern glows,
Guiding souls through veils of night.
Enchanted silence softly flows,
Wrapping all in pure delight.

As dawn approaches, shadows flee,
Light spills forth, a tender start.
In the woods, we find the key,
To the wonders of the heart.

Beneath the Surface

Ripples push, the water stirs,
Whispers deep, a story told.
Secrets hide where vision blurs,
Mysteries, both young and old.

Beneath the waves, the world unfolds,
Pirouetting in hues so bright.
Life abounds in colors bold,
In the depths, the dark takes flight.

Silent currents bear their weight,
Fins that flicker, shadows blend.
Time moves slow, we wait, we wait,
Nature's art, it will not end.

Echoes of a tranquil past,
In the quiet, hearts entwine.
Fleeting moments seem to last,
Beneath the surface, we align.

At twilight's edge, we start to see,
The world above and depths below.
In hidden realms, we long to be,
Where the secrets softly flow.

Veiled in Gloss

Rain-soaked streets, a shiny gloss,
Pavements glimmer in twilight's grace.
Each droplet tells of love and loss,
Mirrored dreams in a still embrace.

City lights begin to blink,
Reflections dance on glassy panes.
Amidst the chaos, we stop to think,
Beauty thrives where the heart remains.

Starlit skies and whispered lies,
Veils of mystery paint the night.
In every smile, a truth belies,
Hopes like shadows take flight.

Winds of change, they softly sigh,
Underneath the silver glow.
Promises made, we reach the high,
In every crack, love's seeds we sow.

Through rain and shine, we carry on,
Veiled in gloss, our spirits rise.
In every dawn, a brand-new song,
Life's reflections are no disguise.

A Whisper of Ice

In the stillness, breath does freeze,
Crystal blades across the ground.
Nature's hush, a sacred tease,
Whispers delicate, profound.

Frosty branches draped in lace,
Every flake a song of light.
Silvery moments we embrace,
In the quiet, pure delight.

A glimmering path of dreams untold,
Where the wild heart learns to glide.
Embracing winter's tender hold,
On this journey, hearts abide.

Glistening echoes, shadows play,
In this world of fragile grace.
A gentle touch, the light of day,
Finds its way, a warm embrace.

With every pulse, the ice will melt,
Underneath a sunlit sky.
As seasons change, new warmth is felt,
A whisper of ice says goodbye.

Echoes of a Silent Night

Whispers of the stars above,
Float softly through the air.
Moonlight casts a silver glow,
As shadows dance in pairs.

The nightingale sings low and sweet,
Threads of magic start to weave.
In shadows deep, dreams take flight,
Where silence dares to believe.

Beneath the cloak of velvet skies,
Time stands still, a gentle pause.
Each heartbeat echoes softly here,
In peace, we find our cause.

A breeze stirs leaves in whispered tones,
Nature's lullaby unfolds.
The world awakens, yet remains,
In stories yet untold.

Together we embrace the night,
With every star, a wish ignites.
Through echoes soft and light as air,
Our dreams soar high to heights.

Through the Crystal Veil

A glimmer forms beyond the haze,
Where shadows mingle at the seams.
Through the crystal veil, we gaze,
Chasing lightly woven dreams.

Reflections dance on liquid ground,
Each ripple sings of tales unseen.
A symphony of silence sound,
In luster bright, a world serene.

The light spills forth in colors bold,
Beneath the arch of azure blue.
From every crease, a secret told,
Of skies reborn as morning dew.

With every step upon this path,
We trace the spark of countless fates.
Through the crystal veil, we laugh,
In wonder where adventure waits.

United by the threads of light,
We weave a tapestry of time.
Through the crystal veil, we rise,
In harmony, our spirits climb.

Shimmers Beneath the Silent Canopy

In twilight's grasp, the forest breathes,
With each leaf, a story flows.
Shimmers gleam as daylight leaves,
Amidst the hush, the soft wind blows.

Beneath the boughs, shadows conspire,
With secrets held in gentle folds.
A lullaby of leaves inspires,
As night unveils its whispered golds.

The stars peek through like shy-eyed dreams,
While silver beams caress the ground.
The world transforms, or so it seems,
As nature sings, profound, unbound.

In this embrace of twilight's swoon,
Where light and darkness gently meet,
Each breath a melody, a tune,
An echo shared in perfect beat.

Let silence reign, and peace align,
In harmony, the soul's delight.
Beneath the canopy divine,
We find our home in endless night.

In the Realm of the Cold Wind

A whisper chills, the cold winds call,
Through barren trees and frost-bound air.
In shadows cast, we stand so small,
Among the echoes, silent, bare.

The moon hangs high, a watchful eye,
Over the fields of silver glow.
As night unfolds, the spirits fly,
In dreams of frost, where memories flow.

Among the stars, we trace our path,
Through icy realms of twilight's breath.
In the stillness, we feel the wrath,
Of winter's grip, a dance of death.

Yet, in this cold, a beauty thrives,
As every flake begins to glow.
In frigid winds, a warmth survives,
Tales of love and life, bestowed.

So let the world freeze, let it still,
In the realm where the cold winds wend.
We'll gather light, our hearts to fill,
And find a way to boldly mend.

Glacial Thoughts

In silence deep, I wander wide,
Where icy winds and sorrows bide.
Thoughts wander like the falling snow,
In glacial paths, my heart does flow.

Each breath a crystal, bright and clear,
In winter's grasp, I know no fear.
Fragments of dreams, they swirl and spin,
Like frozen whispers ghosting in.

The world is hushed, a frosty gleam,
Lost in this cold, I softly dream.
Echoes of warmth begin to fade,
In glacial thoughts, my heart's remade.

Time stands still in this icy realm,
Where shadows dance, and I overwhelm.
In shivers deep, my feelings lie,
As chill and comfort intertwine.

Through frigid nights, the starlight glows,
Embracing all these glacial woes.
In frozen moments, truth is found,
A tranquil heart, in silence bound.

A Dance of Frost and Fog

In twilight's glow, the chill descends,
A dance of frost where silence bends.
The fog rolls in, a veiled surprise,
A waltz unfolds beneath gray skies.

Each breath a mist, a fleeting grace,
As nature spins in soft embrace.
Footsteps hush on the frosted ground,
In this slow dance, peace is found.

Shadows whisper, secrets shared,
In softest fog, no heart is scared.
Together we glide, on winter's stage,
Frost and fog, a timeless page.

The stars peek through the curtain's seam,
Illuminating what we dream.
With frozen hearts, we twirl and sway,
In the cool embrace of winter's play.

A symphony of twinkling light,
As frosty breath takes flight at night.
Together we dance, forever free,
In a world awash with memory.

Moonlight on a Blanket of Snow

Beneath a sky of shining white,
The moon bewitches, silver bright.
A blanket soft, the world aglow,
In this frozen embrace, time flows slow.

Whispers of dreams ride the night air,
On snowflakes' wings, they drift with care.
Each twinkle sparkles, a secret kept,
In serene silence, nature's slept.

Footprints lace the untouched ground,
While shadows dance, without a sound.
The moon holds court, so pure, so high,
Gently watching as moments sigh.

With every glimmer, hearts align,
In this magical chill, love's design.
A tapestry of white and light,
Guiding us through the tranquil night.

Time stands still in this frosty bliss,
A lunar kiss, a tender wish.
Wrap me in warmth, this glow we share,
In moonlight's arms, we breathe the air.

In the Grip of Frost

The morning breaks in frosty hues,
As nature dons her crystal shoes.
In winter's grip, the world turns bright,
A tapestry of pure delight.

Each breath released, a cloud of mist,
In icy realms, we can't resist.
The biting chill, it grips so tight,
Yet in this cold, there's warmth and light.

Frozen landscapes stretch and gleam,
A postcard caught within a dream.
Together we explore the scene,
In laughter's warmth, we find our sheen.

Whispers of winter dance around,
As frosty fingers touch the ground.
Through shadows deep, the sunlight peeks,
A fleeting warmth, the heart it seeks.

In every flake, a story told,
In winter's embrace, we find the bold.
Together we weave through icy gales,
In the grip of frost, our love prevails.

Frigid Beauty

In whispers cold, the silence reigns,
A world adorned in icy chains.
Each breath released, a cloud of white,
As nature dreams in tranquil night.

Trees stand tall, their limbs embraced,
By frost that time has softly traced.
The moonlight dances on frozen streams,
Awakening the winter's dreams.

The stars above, a distant glow,
Reflecting on the pure white snow.
A stillness echoes, softly weaves,
A tapestry that winter leaves.

Crystals form on windows bright,
Transforming day to starlit night.
Each flake a kiss, so sweet and rare,
A frigid beauty, beyond compare.

In this embrace of bitter chill,
The heart finds warmth, the soul finds thrill.
For in the cold, there lies a spark,
Of life and light within the dark.

The Crystal Canvas

Nature paints with icy brush,
Creating scenes where moments rush.
Each flake a gem, a fleeting sight,
Captured in the soft twilight.

On branches bare, the crystals cling,
Each sparkling drop a secret spring.
Glistening under the pale moon's gaze,
A wonder that forever stays.

The frozen lake, a glassy sea,
Reflects the world for all to see.
With every glimmer, life anew,
A canvas bright in shades of blue.

Whispers of winds, a gentle call,
In the stillness, beauty sprawls.
With every breath, each moment true,
The canvas shifts in vibrant hue.

In this realm, where silence sings,
The crystal art of winter clings.
A masterpiece both stark and clear,
In every glance, the heart draws near.

Shadows of the Frost

In shadows deep where frost does creep,
The world lies still, the air is steep.
The night unfolds its icy cloak,
In whispers soft, the secrets spoke.

Beneath the stars, the ground a sheen,
A glimmering coat, a jeweled scene.
With every step, the crunch of snow,
Echoes tales from long ago.

Frost-kissed leaves in twilight's glow,
Softly whisper where no winds blow.
A dance of shadows, gray and bright,
In the embrace of winter's night.

Creeping shapes in silvered light,
Blend with dreams of endless night.
For every shadow holds a tale,
Of beauty wrapped in winter's veil.

While the earth sleeps, wrapped in white,
The heart finds warmth, the soul takes flight.
In frozen shadows, life renews,
In every breath, a chance to choose.

Barren Elegance

In winter's grasp, the branches sigh,
As whispers dance in the cobalt sky.
Barren hills in their quiet grace,
Embrace the chill with soft embrace.

Blankets of snow, a muted hue,
Cover the earth, a tranquil view.
Each step a crunch, in stillness found,
Elegance echoes all around.

The sun, a pearl, in pale ascent,
Glistens on fields, a fleeting moment spent.
Shapes of frost, like lace they lie,
Nature's art, against the sky.

Amidst the stark, there blooms a hint,
Of beauty pure, a gentle glint.
For in the barren, life holds tight,
A promise waiting, hidden from sight.

In silence deep, the heart shall know,
The elegance of winter's show.
Beneath the frost, a world awaits,
A dance of life that never hesitates.

The Quietude of a Snowbound Heart

In winter's grasp, the world lies still,
Each flake a whisper, soft and chill.
Beneath the weight of silent white,
A heart finds peace in the frozen night.

Branches bare, their stories told,
In the quiet, warmth unfolds.
A breath of frost, a breath of air,
In this stillness, love lays bare.

Footsteps light on powdered ground,
In the hush, lost dreams are found.
Every heartbeat, a silent song,
In the snow, we all belong.

The stars peek through clouds above,
In the silence, echoes of love.
A snowbound heart, forever free,
In quietude, it longs to be.

Embraced by peace, the night so deep,
In the tranquil, we find our sleep.
Let the world outside be gray,
In this heart, warmth finds its way.

Fragments of a Shivering Sky

Clouds drift softly, shadows wane,
Fragments dance in a silver rain.
The horizon whispers tales untold,
Of a shivering sky, both fierce and bold.

Sunset spills in hues of fire,
Each glimmer sparks a heart's desire.
Yet twilight's chill begins to creep,
In this beauty, sorrows seep.

Stars awaken, shy and bright,
Their twinkle warms the cloak of night.
In each flicker, hope takes flight,
In fragments, we find the light.

The moon weaves dreams through tangled air,
In shadows cast, we seek to share.
A shivering sky offers grace,
In its embrace, we find our place.

Yet as dawn breaks, colors fade,
In morning's glow, our fears evade.
Each fragment holds a timeless tale,
In the sky's depth, we set our sail.

Translucent Hues of Solitude

In quiet corners, colors blend,
Translucent shades, where soft hearts mend.
Solitude whispers through every tone,
In hidden spaces, we find our own.

A gentle breeze through the willow sways,
In its dance, solitude plays.
Each leaf that falls, a story shared,
Of moments quiet, of hearts laid bare.

Canvas spread beneath the sky,
Painted whispers, the mind can fly.
In hues of blue, a balm for pain,
Translucent dreams fall like rain.

Reflections caught in gentle streams,
In solitude, life's tender dreams.
Each ripple circles, softly spreads,
In fragile peace, where silence treads.

And as the daylight fades away,
Translucent night begins to play.
In solitude's embrace, we find,
The inner strength of a tranquil mind.

Shadows of the Shivering Trees

In twilight's glow, the trees stand tall,
Shadows stretch and softly fall.
Whispers rustle through the leaves,
In their silence, the heart believes.

Roots deep-set in earthen ground,
In their embrace, strength is found.
Branches dance with every breeze,
Shadows play among the trees.

Moonlight filters through the night,
Casting silver, soft and bright.
Each shadow tells a story true,
Of all the dreams that once we knew.

The shivering trunks, a timeless sight,
Keeping secrets of day and night.
In stillness, they hold grace and power,
Witness to each fleeting hour.

As dawn approaches, shadows fade,
In waking light, new paths are laid.
Yet in the dusk, when still we roam,
The trees echo our search for home.

Frozen Reflections

In the stillness, silence hums,
Crystal echoes, a soft drum.
Winter's breath upon my skin,
Mirrored shadows, where dreams begin.

Whispers linger, soft and light,
Glimmers of day fade into night.
Footprints lost in the frosty haze,
Moments captured in a frozen gaze.

World on pause, time stands still,
Chilled air carries a quiet thrill.
Nature's canvas, purest white,
Reflections dance in soft moonlight.

Beneath the ice, life waits and sleeps,
Ancient secrets, the stillness keeps.
Silent stories, soft and deep,
In frozen moments, memories seep.

With every breath, the frost takes flight,
Each glistening flake, a pure delight.
In this landscape, tranquil and wide,
Frozen reflections, time's gentle guide.

Shimmering Frost

Morning glows with a silver sheen,
Frosted patterns, nature's queen.
Sunlight dances on icy blades,
Shimmering beauty, a world remade.

Every twig wears a crystal crown,
The earth adorned, in white spun gown.
A gentle touch, the chill bestows,
Magic woven, as winter grows.

Footfalls crunch on the frozen ground,
In this silence, peace is found.
A moment trapped, in time's embrace,
Shimmering frost, a fleeting grace.

With every breath, the world awakes,
Chasing sunlight, as laughter breaks.
Nature's art, so fresh and bold,
Shimmering tales of winter told.

As shadows stretch and colors play,
Frosty whispers greet the day.
In beauty's grasp, we find our place,
With shimmering frost, life's tender grace.

Echoes of the Chill

In the depths of the frozen air,
Whispers echo, treading bare.
Frostbitten trees, a stark silhouette,
Memories linger that won't forget.

Snowflakes twirl like dancers bright,
Each one a story of pure delight.
Chilled hands warm around the flame,
Echoes whisper, nature's name.

The world slows down in soft repose,
Underneath the icy clothes.
Silence sings a gentle tune,
Echoing softly, morning's boon.

Each breath a cloud, a fleeting sigh,
In the quiet, the heart will fly.
Echoes linger, a tender thrill,
In the peace of the winter chill.

As night descends with its velvet cloak,
Stars awaken, gently provoke.
In frozen moments, dreams take flight,
Echoes of chill, in the quiet night.

Crystal Veil

A shimmering dance, the light unfolds,
Nature's secrets in crystal molds.
Veils of frost drape every scene,
Winter's kiss, a soft routine.

Each branch adorned with sparkling lace,
In this wonder, we find our place.
A breath of magic fills the air,
In the stillness, we pause and stare.

The world transformed, a dazzling sight,
Through the crystal veil, pure and bright.
Footsteps whisper on the frozen ground,
In every heartbeat, beauty's found.

Time slows down, we lose our way,
In the magic of winter's play.
With every glance, new wonders reveal,
In a landscape wrapped in a crystal veil.

As twilight falls, the magic grows,
Underneath the snow, a warmth flows.
In the frosty air, dreams swirl and sail,
Lost in the beauty of a crystal veil.

The Silence of a Snow-Clad World

In the hush of falling snow,
Everything slows to a soft glow.
Nature wraps in a white cloak,
Silence speaks, while shadows soak.

Trees stand tall, their branches bare,
Crystals glisten in the cold air.
Footsteps muffled, whispers fade,
In this peace, a world is made.

The sky wears a gentle gray,
As evening meets the falling day.
Stars peek down, bright and clear,
In this stillness, dreams appear.

Time stretches in the frosty night,
Wrapped in wonder, wrapped in light.
A blanket thick, no sound to find,
In the silence, hearts unwind.

Frozen ponds like mirrors gleam,
Reflecting truths we dare to dream.
In the snow-clad world we roam,
Find in silence, a sense of home.

Facets of the Frosted Hour

Through the window, crystals cling,
Frosted edges on the spring.
Hourglass filled with snowy grace,
Every flake, a delicate trace.

Twilight dances on the frost,
Moments captured, never lost.
Breath hangs in the chilled air,
Time suspended, moments rare.

Shadows creep as daylight wanes,
Whispers floating on cold veins.
Each tick feels like a dream,
Life unfolds in frozen stream.

Glints of silver in dusky light,
A world transformed, quiet and bright.
Listen closely, hear the sound,
Of beauty found beneath the ground.

In this realm where cold is king,
Nature hums, and the night sings.
Facets of a world anew,
In the frost, find more than few.

The Subtle Art of Ice

In a world where shadows play,
Ice sculptures form and sway.
Beneath the skin, the depth is clear,
Nature's hand, so bold yet sheer.

Glistening trails on pathways laid,
Frozen echoes of joy displayed.
Each shard, a story, each edge, a sigh,
Art in nature, standing by.

Gentle streams beneath the freeze,
Flowing softly, whispering ease.
Nature carves with quiet might,
Embracing stillness, dancing light.

The subtle art that speaks in frost,
In every layer, love embossed.
Ribbons of cold that intertwine,
Capture moments, yours and mine.

As dawn breaks, the light will spill,
Transforming ice with gentle thrill.
Yet in those fragile pieces found,
Lies the heart of beauty, profound.

Whispers Beneath the Chill

In the quiet of the night,
Whispers dance in silver light.
Cold winds weave through the trees,
Carrying secrets on the breeze.

Pale moon casts a gentle glow,
Softening edges of the snow.
Nature sighs, a breath so deep,
In the stillness, spirits leap.

Beneath the chill, the earth lies still,
Dreams awaiting, hopes to fill.
Each flake that drifts holds a tune,
Echoes of winter's quiet rune.

Firelight flickers in distant homes,
Warmth and laughter as twilight roams.
Yet out in the cold, a beauty brews,
Whispers calling to the muse.

As dawn arrives with amber hues,
The whispers fade as warmth ensues.
Yet in the quiet, we recall,
The magic held in winter's thrall.

Milton Keynes UK
Ingram Content Group UK Ltd.
UKHW010233111224
452348UK00011B/721